Peter Berger Mayala Mukanzi

Termination of the employment contract: cases of unfair dismissal

Peter Berger Mayala Mukanzi

Termination of the employment contract: cases of unfair dismissal

ScienciaScripts

Imprint

Any brand names and product names mentioned in this book are subject to trademark, brand or patent protection and are trademarks or registered trademarks of their respective holders. The use of brand names, product names, common names, trade names, product descriptions etc. even without a particular marking in this work is in no way to be construed to mean that such names may be regarded as unrestricted in respect of trademark and brand protection legislation and could thus be used by anyone.

Cover image: www.ingimage.com

This book is a translation from the original published under ISBN 978-613-8-43149-7.

Publisher:
Sciencia Scripts
is a trademark of
Dodo Books Indian Ocean Ltd. and OmniScriptum S.R.L publishing group

120 High Road, East Finchley, London, N2 9ED, United Kingdom
Str. Armeneasca 28/1, office 1, Chisinau MD-2012, Republic of Moldova, Europe
Printed at: see last page
ISBN: 978-620-6-22544-7

Table of contents :

EPIGKAPHY

"I know that for humans, perfection is impossible, but excellence is. So do your job, and do it as well as you can, accepting the inevitable mistakes".

MAYALA MUKANZI Peter Berger

DEDICATION

To my very dear mother LENZA KISAMBU Pétronelle, who despite the many socio-economic difficulties contributed to my studies.

Amon pèreBERNARD   MAYALA, for all the confidence and motivation.

To my brothers and sisters MAYALA, RACHEL, DOUDOU, AUGY, HEDER, DANIEL, GRETA and Grâce for their attachment to our memory.

To my alter ego CLARISSE BATUAMBA, for his emotional and moral support.

FOREWORD

On the threshold of this study, which marks the end of our law degree, we are delighted to extend our heartfelt thanks to all those who have contributed to its preparation.

Our special thanks go to Professor BUKA eKa NGOY, who kindly took on the task of directing the study, and through him, to Project Manager ILONGA WENDE Gustave, who, despite their multiple occupations, did not fail to provide us with comments and guidance that were invaluable in helping us to finalize our study.

We are also very grateful to all the members of our university's academic and scientific bodies for the training we received.

May our fellow students NGIENGO MBEMBA, thank God for MAKOLA, God for MOKE, Nickel KIWEY, David MUZEMBA, Reagan MAFUTA, Gabriella KALALA and Guelord LOWOKO, for the moment of faith they shared.

Finally, we would like to thank all those who helped us in any way in the writing of this work, whose names are not quoted. May they find here the expression of our deep and sincere gratitude.[1]

---

[129] Art 149 al 3,3 of the Labor Code
[30] MASANGA PHOBA, op cit

INTRODUCTION

I. Purpose of the study

Not everyone is lucky enough to be an independent entrepreneur. To meet the needs of life, salaried employment remains the only way to go. However, it must be recognized that the weak position of the worker in relation to his employer can expose him to a number of hazards, to the realities of exploitation and modification on the part of the latter. This danger, which is far from platonic, has led to the need to regulate hiring, to devote several provisions to the contract under which it is carried out, and to adopt several provisions, most of which protect the worker, notably those relating to termination of the contract, the examination of which will constitute the subject of our work.

Work, being a biblical recommendation, remains one of man's first-choice activities. Christianity has given work a noble dimension. Work ennobles man, restores his dignity and elevates him. Now is not the time for inertia, wait-and-see attitude or excessive divine interventionism, because manna from heaven belongs to a bygone era. The word work means action, activity, tilled. As the importance of work no longer needs to be demonstrated, various legislations around the world have seen the urgent need to establish the right to work as a fundamental right. Such is the case in the D.R.C.

From the outset, Congolese law has sought to protect workers against the powers of the employer. But this right to work would only be an illusion if it were not accompanied by protection resulting from public measures against the economic and social hardship into which illness, maternity, industrial accidents, death etc.... would plunge workers.

This protection manifests itself through the provisions of international texts and the various legislative and regulatory acts governing the relationship between workers against the various dangers that threaten their rights. The DRC constitution of February 18, 2006, as amended and supplemented by law n°11/002 of 2011, advocates job stability.

In order to ensure this stability, Congolese law no. 15/2002 of October 16, 2002 on the labor code stipulates that "an indeterminate contract may only be terminated at the employer's initiative for a valid reason related to the employee's fitness or conduct at the workplace in the performance of his duties, or based on the operational requirements of the company or department.

Article 63, paragraph 3 of the aforementioned law stipulates that termination of an open-ended contract without just cause entitles the employee to reinstatement. In the absence of such reinstatement, the worker is entitled to damages fixed by the labor court, taking into account in particular the nature of the services rendered, the worker's seniority in the company, his age, and rights acquired in any capacity whatsoever".

Unjustified or unfair dismissal is a reality, not just a hypothetical situation. These will be the focus of this paper, with particular emphasis on unfair dismissal through termination of an employer's employment contract.

II. Interest of the subject

All scientific work has a foundation, a justification, in short, an interest. Ours is no exception. Work has many virtues. It prevents idleness, which is rightly said to be the mother of all vices, and to a large extent ensures public safety, improves living conditions, contributes to the creation of income and thus promotes the country's development. It must therefore be protected, as stipulated in article 36 of our constitution, to the benefit of all parties, especially those in a weak position. This work will have the great merit of popularizing the way in which this function is carried out, while emphasizing the provisions relating to the termination of contracts decided on alternatively, pointing out any weaknesses and proposing, if necessary, the appropriate remedies for the greatest efficiency.

III. Methodology

All scientific work requires an appropriate method. Method is the set of intellectual operations by which a discipline seeks to reach the truths it pursues, demonstrates and verifies them, or an intellectual approach required by the appropriate theoretical scheme in order to explain a series of observed phenomena[2] .

In order to get to the heart of this study, we will use two methods:

---

[2] Grawitz and PINTO, Methods of social sciences, Ed. Dalloz, Paris 1977

exegetical and sociological.

The exegetical approach will lead us to collect, interpret and analyze the legal instruments relating to the chosen subject.

As for the second, the sociological method has given us the opportunity to compare the disputes recorded. It will also enable us to analyze a number of judicial decisions to see how unfair dismissals are perceived and punished in our country.

IV. Summary plan

In addition to the introduction and conclusion, our work will be subdivided into three chapters:

- The first will provide a general overview of the employment contract. It will be divided into three sections. The first will focus on its definition, form, proof and duration. The second will focus on its characteristics and conditions, while the last section will compare it with neighbouring conventions.

- The second will cover the end of this contract. It will be divided into two sections. The first will deal with common causes, and the second with specific causes for termination of the contract under study.

- The last section deals with unfair dismissal and its effects. It will naturally be subdivided into two sections. The first will be devoted to unfair dismissal and the second to its effects.

CHAPTER I. GENERAL OVERVIEW OF THE EMPLOYMENT CONTRACT

This chapter will define the concept of the employment contract, indicate the form, proof and duration of the employment contract, the procedures for proving the contract and, finally, determine the duration of the contract and the difference between the employment contract and related agreements.

Section I: DEFINITION, FORM, EVIDENCE AND DURATION

§1 . The definition

Employment contracts used to be called "louage de service" (hire of service) under articles 37O to 427 of the Congolese Civil Code, Book III, as well as article 1er of the decree-law of February 21, 1967 on contracts for the hire of services[3] .

The Congolese legislator defines an employment contract as "any agreement, written or verbal, by which one person, the worker, undertakes to provide another person, the employer, with manual or other work under the direct or indirect direction and authority of the latter and in return for remuneration"[4] .

Three essential elements emerge: performance, subordination and remuneration.

---

[3] KUMBU KI NGIMBI, cours de droit du travail, notes for L1 students (Congolese universities), law, Kin, January 2009
[4] Art 7.C of law n°015/2002 of October 16, 2002 on the labor code, as amended and supplemented by law n°16/010 of July 15, 2016.

For KIYALA, "the contract of employment is the agreement by which a person undertakes to place his activity at the disposal of another person, under whose direction he places himself, in return for remuneration.[5]

We can say that this definition takes up the bases on which this contract rests, but we give the quality of the parties, which constitutes a small weakness.

From the foregoing, we say that the contract of employment is a synallagmatic, onerous, consensual, successive contract involving the provision of work in return for remuneration under the authority and direction of another person, the employer.

Let's move on to the form of this contract.

§2 . The shape

This contract under study must at least be drafted in the form that suits the parties. It must, however, include the information specified in article 212 of the French Labor Code:

- employer's name or company name ;
- employer's INSS registration number;
- the last name, first name(s), middle name(s) and sex of the worker;
- the worker's date of birth or, failing that, the nullissimo of the presumed year, etc. ....

---

[5] KIYALA, teaching manual for the labor law course, I1 Law, UNIBAND, 2015-2016

Except in the case of day-to-day contracts, the employment contract must be drawn up in French, in at least four copies, and signed by both parties. If one of the parties is unable to sign, he or she may affix a fingerprint[6].

§3 . The proof

As employment contracts must normally be evidenced by a written document drawn up in the appropriate form, they can be proven by any legal means.

Written form is the normal form required, but it may also be verbal, a possibility which is also included in the definition.

The written form, the proof, poses no problem, it is done on its simple presentation.

If this is not the case, the employee can use any legal means to establish not only the existence of the content of the agreement, but also any subsequent changes made to it.[7]

In the absence of any of the information specified in the aforementioned article 212 of the French Labor Code, the employee's declarations are taken into consideration until proven otherwise. Subsequent changes in the employee's social situation are deemed to be incorporated into the employment contract, provided they have been duly

---

[6] Art 4 of Ministerial Order no. 062/cab/PVPM/ETPS/2011 of July 22, 2011 establishing the form, proof and visa of the employment contract.
[7] Article 49 of the Labor Code

notified to the employer[8] .

After the proof, in the next section we'll give you the essentials about the duration of this contract.

§4 . Duration

All employment contracts are either fixed-term or open-ended[9] .

All employment contracts are either fixed-term or open-ended. This is what we will analyze in the following lines.

A. Fixed-term contract

Under the terms of article 40 al 1 of the French Labor Code, "a fixed-term contract is one which is concluded either for a specific period of time, or for a specific task, or for the replacement of a worker who is temporarily unavailable". Such a contract necessarily implies the indication in the contract of a fixed date or event, after which the parties are discharged of their mutual obligations, unless tacitly renewed.

In other words, to qualify as a fixed-term contract, the term or expiry date chosen by the parties must be certain as to when it will occur.

In practice, this form is often used by seasonal industries (hotels) and agriculture (employees hired for a specific job).

Article 41 paragraph 1 of the Labor Code stipulates that "the duration of this

---

[8] MASANGA PHOBA, COURS DE DROIT DU TRAVAIL, L1 DROIT, UNikin, 2016-2017, unpublished
[9] Art 39 of the Labor Code

contract may not exceed two years. This period may not exceed one year if the worker is married and separated from his family, or is widowed, legally separated or divorced and separated from his children for whom he is responsible.

However, in certain circumstances, a fixed-term contract loses its status and is deemed to have been concluded for an indefinite period.

At present, a fixed-term contract presupposes the existence of a definite term guaranteeing job stability and justifying the absence of notice periods. In addition to fixed-term contracts, we will now discuss open-ended contracts in the following section.

B. Open-ended contract

The legislator is silent on the definition, but simply states that when the worker is hired to occupy a permanent position in the company or establishment, the contract must be concluded for an indefinite period.

According to a certain doctrine, "an employment contract is said to be open-ended when the parties have not specified exactly or indirectly the duration of the engagement".

Unlike the above-mentioned fixed-term contract, an open-ended contract is one without a fixed term. However, the decree of July 30, 1888 on contracts or conventional obligations prohibits a lifetime commitment; it is therefore possible to break the contractual link by giving notice.

In fact, the Congolese legislator is much more in favor of open-ended contracts, which guarantee job stability, as recommended by article 36 of the Congolese constitution of February 18, as revised to date.

This is why, as mentioned above, certain facts make a contract deemed to be of indeterminate duration. These include

- When the worker is hired to fill a permanent position in the company or establishment;

- Where a contract concluded for a fixed term in breach of the provisions of article 42 al 1 of the Labour Code ;

- When the worker concludes more than 2 fixed-term contracts with the same employer or company, or renews a fixed-term contract more than once;

- When the fixed-term contract exceeds two years.

In fact, Congolese law is much more in favor of open-ended contracts, which guarantee job stability, as recommended by article 36 of the Congolese constitution of February 18, as revised to date. Work is not only a right, but also a duty, since it is the means by which goods are produced and distributed, and services provided. As such, it is not only an asset for economic development, but also a social guarantee.

On the other hand, it can be argued that an employment contract will be so qualified if the parties have not specified the exact or indirect duration of the engagement. This would be the case if a fixed-term contract was concluded in violation of the relevant legal provisions.

After examining the definition, form and proof of an employment contract, the following section examines its characteristics and conditions of validity.

SECTION 2 CHARACTERISTICS AND CONDITIONS

§1 . The characters

A. Consensual character

As we have already alluded to, the contract under examination is consensual, synallagmatic, for valuable consideration, successive and intuitu personae.

A contract is consensual because it is formed solely by the will of the parties. It results from the exchange of the parties' consents, the employer's offer and the worker's acceptance.

B. Synallagmatic nature

The employment contract is a synallagmatic contract, since it creates reciprocal obligations for the parties. One performs the agreed work (the worker) and the other pays the agreed salary (the employer). In the words of the legislator, it is commutative in that each of the parties undertakes to give or deal something which is considered to be the equivalent of what he is given or owes for it.[10]

---

[10] Article 4 of CCCL III

C. For valuable consideration

An employment contract is a contract for pecuniary gain, as each party derives a benefit from the contract. There is therefore a counterparty for each party. It is the one that obliges each party to give or do something.[11]

D. Successive character

Whether a fixed-term or open-ended contract, the obligations arising from the contract are staggered over time. They are performed successively, not instantaneously.

E. Character intuitu Personae

In addition to the above-mentioned characteristics, the employment contract is also intuitu personae, since it is concluded in consideration of the worker's person, i.e. his or her skills and certain other criteria which give rise to a presumption on the part of the employer of correct and irreproachable performance of the tasks to be carried out by him or her. This is why, in the event of the worker's death, none of his heirs or successors can claim a replacement. It is in a personal capacity that the employee has been hired by the employer to work for the company. The situation of one or the other is totally different. As the company is an economic unit, any changes in name or ownership require the contract to be renewed between new employers and staff.

---

[11] Art 4 of CCCL III

Now it's time to move on to the second paragraph concerning the conditions of validity of this contract.

§2 . Conditions of validity

Like other contracts, and despite the rules specific to them, employment contracts are subject to the rules of common law in terms of form and substance[12] .

A. Substantive conditions

The substantive conditions are those set out in article 8 of Book III of the Congolese Civil Code: consent, capacity, certain object and lawful cause.

1.   Expressing consent

The concomitant manifestation after free discussion as the basis is the moral, economic and legal justification for the binding force of the commitment entered into.

This concept needs to be clarified in the case of individual employment relationships, since the expression of will is in most cases unilateral in nature, emanating from the employer who imposes his conditions. It is also collective in the sense that an identical charter of working conditions is instituted by the employer for all the company's

---

[12] Art. 8 of the decree law of July 30, 1888 op. cit.

employees.

The employee's consent is tacitly given in two stages: at the time of hiring and during the term of the contract. This is what allows the application of article 33 of CCCLIII.

2. Characteristics of consent

Necessity of the employee's personal consent. The emphasis here is on the employee's ability to give consent.

Consent must be free from defects (error, fraud, violence and injury).

Definitive consent required. The issue of definitive consent is linked to the problem of probationary employment (Art. 43 of Act no. 015, Labour Code).

As stated above, an employment contract, like any other contract, requires the consent of the parties. They must consent to the conclusion of the contract. Often, however, the worker's position of weakness in relation to his employer gives the contract the appearance of a contract of adhesion. Either he accepts the conditions proposed by the latter alone, or those set out in the collective agreement, if any, and the contract is formed, or he rejects them and there is no contract. Whatever we may observe in practice, the legislator wants this consent to be both free and consensual: it cannot be given through fraud or error, nor can it be extorted by violence.

In this respect, the probationary clause can prove useful, as it enables the employer to make an objective judgment of the employee's competence and suitability for the job in question. During this period, the employee will check whether the task entrusted to him or her is suitable.

We should point out, however, that error only vitiates a contract when it concerns the substance of the thing itself which is the object of the contract, and in the case of violence, when it is of such a nature as to make an impression on a reasonable person and may inspire fear of exposing his person to considerable and present harm.[13]

3. Capacity

In the case of salaried employment, the legislator has introduced special rules for married women and minors, while today only the former are subject to marital authorization. This is due to the combined interpretation of articles 6 of law no. 015/2002 of October 16 on the labor code and article 44 of law no. 87/010 of August 1987 on the family code.

Today, it is freed from this constraint with the amendment made to the Labor Code by Law n°16/010 of July 15, 2016. Indeed, it defines a worker as "any natural person of contracting age regardless of sex, marital status or nationality who undertakes to place his or her professional activity for remuneration under the responsibility and authority of another natural person or legal entity.[14]

In our country, the minimum age for employment is 18[15] . However,

---

[13] Articles 10 and 11 of CCCL III
[14] Article 7.1 of law n°16/010 of July 15 amending the labor code
[15] Article 6 paragraph 2 of the aforementioned law of July 15

the legislator has made a number of arrangements for minors, and even better for those who do not meet this age requirement.

Thus, a person aged 15 may be hired or retained in service, even as an apprentice, but only with the express authorization of the president of the tribunal de paix, following a psycho-medical opinion. The parents or guardians, or the labour inspector, may object, but the objection may be lifted by the same judicial authority if circumstances and equity justify it.[16]

Persons between the ages of 16 and 18 may only work or be kept at work by express dispensation of the President of the Court of Peace, but only to perform light and sanitary work[17].

People with disabilities, on the other hand, can work when they have all their professional and intellectual aptitudes. Disability is not an obstacle.

4. The purpose and cause of the employment contract

Like any other contract, an employment contract must have a purpose, i.e. to provide a specific service, which must be lawful. It must not concern an activity prohibited by law or outrage public decency.

The cause must exist and obey the same requirements[18].

For the employee, it means the benefit of remuneration, and for the employer, the benefit of an agreed service.

---

[16] Article 6 paragraph 2 point 1 and 3 of the aforementioned law
[17] Article 6 paragraph 2 point 4 op.cit
[18] See in particular articles 25, 26, 27, 30 and 32 of ccclll

Individual qualification is essentially contractual, and must be specified in the employment contract at the time of hiring. Qualification depends on the duties performed by the employee, and the employer is allowed to upgrade but not downgrade a worker.

At the level of the Ministry of Labour, there are 5 categories of workers:

- Labourers: those who carry out work requiring no special knowledge (ordinary labourers and heavy labourers; e.g. sweepers, warehousemen^);
- Specialized laborers: take care of simple jobs that require no special knowledge, but do require some fine-tuning and rapid adaptation (e.g. bailiffs);

- Semi-skilled worker: someone who performs work requiring special knowledge of the trade acquired through partial apprenticeship;
- Skilled workers: those responsible for work requiring knowledge of the trade;
- The highly skilled worker: a worker with in-depth knowledge.

The obligations of the parties to an employment contract must be based on a lawful cause, i.e. one that complies with the law and is not contrary to public policy or morality.

In principle, the employer's obligations arise from the employee's performance. In this case, the payment of remuneration by the employer or the performance of the agreed work cannot be vitiated if it is neither prohibited by law nor contrary to public order and morality.

It's worth pointing out that the French Labor Code sets out a specific condition for a person to be able to validly engage his or her services, namely the obligation to produce a certificate of physical fitness. In other words, fitness for work is a particular condition for a person to validly engage his or her services. This requirement would constitute a limitation on the ability of workers to exercise their profession, with the prior production of a certificate of fitness for work issued by a doctor approved by the employer.

Having reviewed the substantive conditions of an employment contract, it is time to consider the formal conditions in section b below.

B. Formal requirements

This is a tricky point to develop, since on the one hand, the law gives the clear impression of requiring a written document for the validity of this written contract, which must also bear the visa of the ONEM[19] , and on the other, recognizes its intense validity if it is verbal. The position is therefore not clear-cut, but it does indicate the information that must imperatively be included in the contract, or rather the facts and elements on which details must be provided, giving it a certain formality.

Being a consensual contract, it is not subject to any particular form for its validity. It may be concluded in writing or verbally. However, it

---

[19] Article 44 paragraph, 46 and 7 paragraph 1 and 2

must be evidenced in writing and drawn up in the form that suits the parties, as long as it includes the statements set out in article 212 of the Labour Code, namely :

- Civil identity of employer and employee;
- The nature of the services to be provided by the worker ;
- Amount of remuneration ;
- Place(s) of performance ;
- Commitment date ;
- Length of notice ;
- Effective date of contract ;
- Place and date of contract conclusion
- Physical fitness ;
- Employer's INSS registration numbers

It is drawn up in French, in at least four copies, and signed by each of the parties.

It should be noted that in the absence of a written agreement, the contract is presumed until proven otherwise to have been concluded for an indefinite period. However, this does not apply to day-to-day contracts. Moreover, in the case of a day-to-day commitment, writing is not required by law. In the absence of a written document, the contract is deemed to have been concluded for an indefinite period.

This is a favor for the worker, as Congolese legislation provides for the primacy of the open-ended employment contract in articles 39 to 43.

When one of the conditions of validity of an employment contract is lacking (e.g. absence of consent, immoral cause, unlawful purpose, etc.), nullity is the sanction of the substantive rules.

In principle, nullity resulting from a defect in the formation of the contract has retroactive effects in civil law. However, in view of the successive nature of the employment contract and the obvious concern to protect the employee, jurisprudence rejects this retroactive annulment, as asserted by Madame MASANGA PHOBA.

SECTION III: EMPLOYMENT CONTRACTS AND CERTAIN AGREEMENTS AND RELATED SERVICES

It is sometimes difficult to differentiate between employment contracts and similar agreements whose purpose is to provide work in return for payment.

These will necessarily include employment contracts, contracts of enterprise, subcontracting and, finally, the provision of a contribution in kind.

The distinctive criterion of the employment contract, which is the subordinate relationship, leads us to make this distinction.

§1 . The employment contract and the company contract

A contract of enterprise is a contract by which a person undertakes, in return for remuneration, to perform a specific task for another person.[20] In a contract of enterprise, the employee places his or her work capacity at the service of the employer. In this case, the employee is not subordinate to the person entrusting him with the work, but is free to choose the professional techniques he deems most appropriate for the task in hand. In spite of the fact that he is bound by the estimate presented to him by the client, he remains an independent professional in a branch of activity such as carpentry, electricity, plumbing, masonry...

§1.1 he employment contract and the subcontracting contract

Subcontracting is a contract by which an individual or corporate enterprise, which may or may not be part of the portfolio, entrusts the performance of part of its tasks under its responsibility to a private individual or legal entity known as a subcontractor, in return for remuneration.[21]

The subcontractor carries out the task(s) entrusted to him/her independently, according to the organization he/she has set up, without any subordinate relationship with the other party. The subcontractor may also carry out the work requested by his staff himself, rather than personally, as is the case for a subcontractor under a contract of employment.

---

[20] Art 434 to 446 of the decree of 3O/O8/1888, relating to contracts and conventional obligations
[21] Article 2 of law n°008/008 of July 17, 2008 on general provisions relating to the State's commitment to portfolio companies

§3 The employment contract and the provision of a contribution in kind

Confusion often persists when a partner's contribution is a contribution in kind, i.e. a commitment to provide the company with technical and professional knowledge or services.[22]

But even if the contribution does not make the contributor a worker, he remains independent because his contribution constitutes his constitution to the realization of the company's object, in cash and on the same level of equality. The affectio societatis, whose existence conditions the very existence of the company, excludes any contribution from superior to inferior, any subordination of one to the other.[23]

A contribution in kind does not constitute a contract of employment, as the worker carries out an activity on behalf of the company equivalent to that which he has undertaken to carry out as a contribution, occupying a dominant position in the company. An employment contract often stipulates that the employee is to share in the profits, and is encouraged to work to the best of his or her ability[24] . Despite such a stipulation, the worker remains subordinate to his employer. But when a partner contributes his expertise by sharing profits and contributing to losses, he is not bound by a contract of employment in the absence of a subordinate relationship.

---

[22] BUKA eKa NGOY, Droit des sociétés commerciales, UNIBAND, L1droit, 2014-2015, unpublished.
[23] Article 40.3 of the Uniform Act of April 17, 1997, on the law governing commercial companies and economic interest groups, revised on January 30, 2014.
[24] BUKA eKa NGOY, Droit des sociétés commerciales, UNIBAND, L1droit, 2014-2015, unpublished.

A contribution in kind grants the contributor the right to share in the company's profits and losses, whereas in an employment contract, the contributor is entitled only to his remuneration. However, this does not make the contributor a partner. He is not the equal of the founders, but works under their authority.[25]

After this general overview of the employment contract, the following chapter deals with the termination of the employment contract.

[25] BUKA eKa NGOY, op cit

CHAPTER II. TERMINATION OF THE EMPLOYMENT CONTRACT

In this chapter, we will look at the question of the termination of an employment contract, which can result from causes that are either common or specific to each type of employment contract.

As DARANAS STYLIANI writes, the employment contract is the main source of individual employment relationships under the liberal system.[26] The parties are free to commit themselves, but can also withdraw from their obligations.

SECTION I. COMMON CAUSES OF CONTRACT TERMINATION

The following are the causes of dissolution for all employment contracts: death of the worker, death of the employee, death of the employee's spouse, death of the employee's spouse, death of the employee's spouse.

mutual consent, force majeure, gross negligence and inability to perform the contract as a result of illness or accident.

§1 . The death of the worker

The death of an employee definitively terminates the employment contract. This is so obvious that the Labor Code makes no mention of it, nor does it specify the obligations that the employer must assume in the event of this fatal, unavoidable event.[27]

---

[26] Daranas Styliani, Droit du travail et de la sécurité sociale, tome I, L1 Droit UNIKIN, 1999
[27] Masanga PHOBA, _Droit du travail,_ 6th edition, revised and argued, Kinshasa 2011, p 66

Legally, we need to mention this, because the legislator has required the worker to personally perform the work that constitutes the object of his engagement.[28]

This is not a continuation of the contract of the deceased worker, but simply a favor granted to the bereaved family to ensure its survival. The replacement does not necessarily involve the same position, working conditions or remuneration.[29]

§2 Mutual consent

The employment contract is born of the will of the employer and the employee. We must therefore accept that it can be terminated when both parties so decide.

As we can see, the French Labor Code does not contain any provisions on how to revoke a contract for this reason. It only mentions it incidentally in the chapter devoted to travel and transport, stating that the right to a return trip is also acquired at the employer's expense, in proportion to the length of service completed, when the parties terminate the contract by mutual agreement after 12 months' service.[29]

However, there can be no doubt as to the legality of this method of termination, since it remains the very affirmation of the principle of autonomy of will, which holds that parties who have freely committed

---

[28] Article 50 al 1 of the Labour Code
[29] KUMBU -KI- Ngimbi, op cit

themselves (mutus consensus) may freely withdraw (mutus dissensus)[30] .

In our research at the Bandundu High Court, we found that this type of contract termination is rare. Workers feel that the benefits they obtain in the event of dismissal outweigh those that could be granted if the contract were terminated in this way.

§3 Force majeure

Force majeure is the occurrence of   an act of God. unforeseeable, unavoidable and insurmountable, rendering the performance of the employment contract impossible and leading to its suspension or termination, depending on whether or not the event characterizing it is temporary.

Professor KUMBU KI NGIMBI goes further, saying that the fact must be a definitive obstacle to the performance of the employment contract.

By fulfilling the above-mentioned conditions, force majeure terminates employment, and the employer does not have to comply with the dismissal procedure, and cannot be ordered to pay damages for wrongful termination.

In the event of force majeure, the contract may be terminated:

- Fire or natural disaster resulting in the destruction of work premises;
- The worker's inability to perform the duties of his job following long-term detention, illness or death, - Le fait du prince (an act of public authority

making it impossible to perform the employment contract).

A. The effects of force majeure to be retained are :

> For open-ended contracts, the employer notifies the employee of the suspension, and after two months has the right to terminate the contract (Art. 68 in conjunction with Art. 60 point C). The effects of this are: no notice period, no compensation for wrongful termination as it is not attributable to the employer.
>
> In the case of fixed-term contracts, force majeure exonerates the contractor from all liability and compensation for early termination.

§4 La Faute Lourde

We will examine the concept, procedure and effects of gross negligence in turn.

A. The notion

According to article 72 paragraph 2 of the Labor Code," writes NZANGI BATUTU, "a party commits gross negligence when the rules of good faith do not allow the other party to be required to continue to perform the contract.

This definition," adds NZANGI B., "draws its substance from case law, which has consistently affirmed that gross negligence is understood as a fault that makes the immediate continuation of contractual relations impossible. It leads to a deterioration in the relationship between the parties, making it impossible to maintain the contractual link, even for the duration of the notice period.

From the above, we can deduce that gross negligence is the result of the occurrence of a situation of such exceptional gravity as to make it morally impossible for the injured party to tolerate the continuation of the contract.

One party is guilty of gross negligence when, through its own actions, the rules of good faith do not allow it to require the other party to continue to perform the contract.

This definition," adds NZANGI B., "draws its substance from case law, which has consistently affirmed that gross negligence is understood as a fault that renders the immediate continuation of contractual relations impossible. It leads to a deterioration in the relationship between the parties, making it impossible to maintain the contractual link, even for the duration of the notice period.

We can deduce from the above that gross negligence is the result of the occurrence of a situation of exceptional gravity which makes it morally impossible for the injured party to continue the contract.

The Labor Code enumerates a series of acts that may constitute gross misconduct on the part of the employer, namely serious breach of contractual obligations, in particular acts of impropriety, sexual or moral harassment, intimidation, assault, serious insults or toleration of similar acts by other workers, and failure to comply with health and safety regulations.

For the employee, too, the list of grounds for gross negligence is not exhaustive, i.e. compromising the company's safety through carelessness, immoral acts, to name but a few.

B. The procedure Paragraphs 3 and 4 of article 72 state that "the party proposing to terminate the contract for gross negligence must notify the other party of its decision in writing no later than fifteen working days after becoming aware of the facts it is invoking.

For investigative purposes, the employer may notify the employee of the suspension of his or her duties within two working days of the event.

C. The effects of gross negligence

Under article 75 of the Labour Code, if the contract is terminated under one of the provisions of article 73, the employer is ordered to pay the employee damages, which should be determined in accordance with the assessment method set out in article 63 of the Labour Code.

These damages are intended to compensate for the harm caused by the breach of contract defined as "gross negligence" by law, the employment contract, the collective bargaining agreement or company regulations, and not for the harm resulting from the breach itself.

The Labor Code lists a series of acts that may constitute gross misconduct on the part of the employer, namely serious breach of contractual obligations, in particular acts of impropriety, intimidation, sexual or moral harassment, assault, serious insult or tolerance of similar acts by other workers, reduction or deduction from the worker's remuneration, and failure to comply with health and safety regulations[30] .

In the case of the employee, this includes serious breach of contract, such as acts of impropriety, serious insults to the employer or his staff, harassment or assault; intentional damage caused to the employer during or in connection with the performance of the contract; or compromise or recklessness with regard to the safety of the company, the workplace or the staff.[31]

§5 . Inability to perform the contract due to illness or accident

In the case of occupational illness, the contract is suspended if the worker is unable to work for one month. After this period, the worker is placed at the disposal of the national social security institute. On the other hand, in the case of a non-occupational illness, the employment contract is suspended for six months of inability to work. In this case, the employer may terminate the contract in return for compensation equivalent to the notice

---

[30] Article 73 of the Labor Code
[31] Article 74 of the Labor Code

period required for an open-ended contract.

That concludes our discussion of the common grounds for terminating an employment contract. Let's move on to the specific grounds for each form of termination.

SECTION 2. SPECIAL CAUSES

First, we'll look at the specific provisions for fixed-term contracts, and then at those that apply only to the contract itself.

§1 . For fixed-term contracts

For a contract of this nature, termination follows naturally from the expiry of the agreed term. In the words of the law, it terminates on expiry of the term fixed by the parties. This being the case, a clause inserted in such a contract provides for the right to terminate it by operation of law.

As mentioned above, an employment contract is said to be for a fixed term when it is concluded either for a specific period of time, or for the completion of a specific project, or for the replacement of a worker who is temporarily unavailable. The term of the contract is fixed by a future and certain event. It is up to the parties to set the duration of the agreement, subject to the following reservations: You can only engage your services for a specific period of time or for a specific undertaking. This article prohibits a lifetime commitment.

However, Congolese law sets the maximum duration of a fixed-term employment contract at 2 years, which may be renewable once.

Combining articles 69 and 70 of the French Labor Code, we find that there are two ways of terminating a fixed-term employment contract: termination on the agreed date and early termination.

A. Termination on the agreed due date

In principle, a fixed-term employment contract is automatically terminated on expiry. A clause in such a contract providing for termination by notice is automatically null and void.

B. Early retirement

Under the French Labor Code, fixed-term employment contracts cannot be terminated except for gross negligence.

Termination for gross negligence does not give rise to any compensation for the party at fault. It should be noted that termination for gross negligence may be initiated by either the employer or the employee.

On the other hand, if the termination is due to failure to comply with the provisions of article 69 paragraph 2 of the French Labor Code, it gives rise to damages corresponding to the wages and benefits of any kind that the employee would have received during the period remaining until the end of his contract. It is up to the judge to decide whether the facts are sufficiently serious to justify termination of the contract.

Recent doctrine, supported by KIYALA and MASANGA PHOBA,

also suggests that a fixed-term employment contract may be terminated on the grounds of non-performance by one of the parties of its contractual obligations.

This position is defensible not only in view of the synallagmatic nature of the employment contract, but also in accordance with article 82 of CCCLIII, which provides for the implicit existence of a resolutory condition in the event that a party fails to perform its obligations towards its co-contractor.

§2 . For open-ended contracts

An open-ended employment contract can always be terminated at the will of one of the parties, for two reasons: to safeguard individual freedom and to ensure the necessary mobility of the workforce for the company[32] .

It may be terminated by the employee's resignation or by the employer's dismissal.

A. Employee resignation

Resignation is the act by which an employee gives up the exercise of his or her duties. In other words, it is a unilateral act by which an employee on an open-ended contract clearly and unequivocally expresses his or her intention to terminate the contract.

In France, resignation is not expressly regulated by the Labor

---

[32] KIYALA,OP.Cit

Code.[33]

According to legal doctrine, resignation is a unilateral legal act on the part of the employee, implying a clear and unequivocal expression of intent to terminate the contract[34] . Most resignations are for reasons of personal convenience. The employee's right to unilaterally terminate the contract must be exercised in accordance with the procedure laid down by law. This involves notifying the employer of the decision and giving notice.

1. Notification of resignation

Any termination of the contract must be notified in writing by the party taking the initiative. In the absence of a written document, only a serious and unequivocal expression of intent on the part of the employee can justify termination of the employment contract. An employee who leaves his or her post without notifying the employer of his or her decision to terminate the contract, and without giving notice, commits gross misconduct likely to result in his or her being ordered to pay compensation for the damage caused to the employer.[35]

Although a right, resignation cannot be decided to the detriment of the employer.

Thus, an employee who resigns after a six-month training period at the company's expense causes the company material damage in terms of

---

[33] MASANGA PHOBA, op cit, P 83
[34] KIYALA, OP. Cit
[35]

out-of-pocket expenses, not to mention the loss to the company of the results he was expected to achieve after the training received. Such a resignation, tainted by an abuse of rights, can only give rise to compensation for the damage suffered by the employer[36] .

2. Advance notice

When the employee initiates the termination of the contract, he is obliged to give the employer a period of notice equal to half the period of notice that the employer would have given him had the employee initiated the termination. Under no circumstances may the notice period exceed this limit.[37]

For the reader's information, it should be noted that unless a longer period is agreed by the parties to the collective bargaining agreement, the employer's notice period cannot be less than 14 working days from the day following notification. This period is increased by 7 working days for each full year of continuous service counted from date to date.[38] The period thus calculated is reduced by half for notice given by the employee.

B. Retirement

After many years of service, the worker is entitled to a rest period known as "retirement". This entitlement applies to those who have reached the age of 65 for men and 60 for women. Entitlement to a pension is subject

---

[36] MASANGA PHOBA, op.cit.
[37] Article 64 paragraph 2 of the Labor Code
[38] Article 64 op cit

to at least 60 months' insurance. The latest text, dated July 1er 1989, raises the provisional age for entitlement to a retirement pension to 62, but only in the case of men. It is up to the employee to negotiate retirement with the employer, or to decide unilaterally to leave the company. In such cases, it goes without saying that the employee must give the employer the statutory notice required to replace him/her.

However, under French law, employers may, in certain cases, unilaterally retire workers who are entitled to a full-time old-age pension, i.e. under the general scheme, have reached the required age and fulfilled the insurance period condition[39] .

In the Congo, however, reaching retirement age is neither an obligation to grant a pension nor a reason for dismissal; it is merely a right that only the worker is free to exercise[40] .

Should the employee wish to exercise this right at a later date, the employer may only object if, following a medical examination of fitness for work, the employee is found to be unfit to continue working.

C. Redundancy

According to article 62 of the French Labor Code, dismissal is a unilateral decision by the employer to terminate an employee's contract for a valid reason related to fitness or conduct, or based on the needs of the

---

[39] MASANGA PHOBA, op.cit.
[40] MASANGA PHOBA,op.cit

company or department.

An employee must not be dismissed without just cause.

Under no circumstances may a worker be dismissed on the grounds of his or her opinions, ethnic group, race, union membership, sex, etc.

The dismissal of one or more employees on the grounds of individual misconduct or unsuitability constitutes dismissal for personal reasons, often referred to as "individual dismissal",   whereas   the dismissal of one or more employees on the grounds of individual misconduct or unsuitability constitutes dismissal for personal reasons, often referred to as "individual dismissal".

When, for economic reasons or internal company reorganization, the employer decides to dismiss one or more employees from the company at the same time, the dismissal is called "economic redundancy". Redundancies for economic reasons may be individual or collective, depending on whether they involve the departure of one or more employees.

The distinction between individual and collective dismissal should not take into account the number of workers involved. Rather, the distinction is based on the reason for dismissal. Indeed, several workers may be dismissed simultaneously for economic reasons.

It is imperative to distinguish between dismissal for personal reasons and dismissal for economic reasons. But before examining these different motives, it is important to know what exactly constitutes a valid motive. We believe that a valid reason is one that rests on rational grounds, is sufficiently stable and susceptible to verification or proof to the contrary. Establishing the validity of a reason is therefore a matter for the judge to assess on the basis of the facts surrounding the act invoked as grounds for dismissal.

Let's take a look at the various valid reasons for dismissing an employee:

- Dismissal based on employee conduct ;
- Dismissal based on the employee's aptitude ;
- Dismissal for economic reasons.

Employers wishing to terminate an employee's employment for reasons relating to his conduct must notify the employee and then give him a notice period or notice of termination which may not be less than 14 working days from the day following notification. This period is increased by 7 working days for each full year of continuous service counted from date to date. If the termination is initiated by the employee, the period of notice shall be equal to half that which would have been given by the employer. Under no circumstances may it exceed this limit.

N.B.: The 14 days' notice is for manual workers and for supervisory and managerial staff; the notice period is no different from that for manual and other workers.

in accordance with the decree of October 26, 2005 setting the duration and conditions of the notice period.

According to this decree, the notice period is one month, increased by 9 working days for each full year of continuous service counted from date to date for supervisory staff. For supervisors and managers, the notice period is 3 months, increased by 16 working days for each full year of continuous service.

Notification of dismissal must be in writing and sent by the initiating party to the other party, with express indication of the reason when the initiative comes from the employer, which applies to both individual and mass dismissals. Articles 62 and 63 deal with unjustified dismissal, unfair dismissal and the penalties applicable in such cases.

In France, the onus is on each party to provide the judge with evidence to convince him or her, while the judge is responsible for establishing the evidence and making his or her own assessment of whether or not the facts constitute real or serious grounds.

When dismissal appears unfair, the employee does not take the matter directly to court, since in labor matters there is a preliminary phase known as the conciliation phase, which we call the negotiated solution phase before the labor inspector.

It is clear that dismissal is subject to the conditions laid down by law and regulations. In the absence of a valid reason, dismissal is unfair. This last point will be the focus of our final chapter.

We cannot close this chapter without mentioning the reciprocal obligations of each party after termination of the employment contract. We will look successively at the obligations of the employer and those of the employee.

C.1 Employer's obligations

When the employment contract is terminated, the employer is obliged to issue a certificate of termination and a receipt for final payment. The employer must also declare the employee's departure to the labor inspectorate and, if necessary, repatriate the employee or pay for the return trip.

- Delivery of the certificate of completion of services

Under the terms of article 79 of the Labor Code, "when the contract is terminated for any reason whatsoever, the employer is required to issue the worker with a certificate attesting to the nature and duration of the services provided, the date on which the services began and ended, and the worker's registration number with the National Social Security Institute. No other information may be added.

The certificate must be handed in no later than two working days after the end of the contract. It is exempt from stamp duty and registration fees. The work certificate is the document issued at the end of the work contract, providing information on the nature and duration of the services provided, the start and end dates of the services, and the worker's INSS registration number. It follows from this provision that the issue of the certificate of completion of services is a legal obligation, the non-performance or delay in performance of which may give rise to compensation if it is established that the worker has suffered prejudice. It has been ruled that the work certificate is quertible and not portable.

- Issuance of a receipt for final settlement of accounts

Also known as a "reçu pour solde de tout compte", the "quittance pour solde de tout compte" is a written attestation from the employee to the employer at the end of the contract, acknowledging receipt of all outstanding sums. Article 100 of the Labor Code stipulates that "any sums remaining due under an employment contract at the definitive termination of effective services must be paid to the employee and, where applicable, to the latter's dependents, no later than two working days after the date of termination of services". Furthermore, Article 71 of the Labor Code informs us that the quittance pour solde de tout compte, issued to the employee when the certificate expires, does not imply renunciation of his or her rights.

- Filing the declaration of departure with the labor inspectorate

The employer must notify the labor inspectorate of all workers hired within 48 hours. Violation of this obligation may result in a fine. This obligation is not required in the case of day-to-day hiring or the hiring of domestic staff.

- Employee repatriation (return trip)

Repatriation refers to the return journey, defined by the legislator as the distance, at the end of the contract or period of service, from the place of performance of the work to the place of acceptance of the engagement or promise of engagement.

This return journey must be made as soon as possible after the end of the service. However, if the employer fails to fulfil his obligations, the local labour inspector will summon him to do so within 6 days. After this period, the aforementioned authority, acting in place of the employee, will refer the matter to the labour court, without prejudice to the penalties provided for in Title XV of the Labour Code.

C.2 Employee obligations

At the end of the contract, the worker's obligations include returning the work tool and refraining from unfair competition with the employer.

After these general facts about the employment contract and its termination, the next chapter deals with unfair dismissal and its effects.

CHAPTER III. UNFAIR DISMISSAL AND ITS EFFECTS

As its title makes clear, this final chapter of our study will be divided into two sections.

The first deals with unfair dismissal and the second with its effects.

SECTION 1. UNFAIR DISMISSAL

We are going to define this notion and distinguish it from illegal dismissal.

§1 . The notion

It should be noted that the French Labor Code does not use the term "abusive dismissal", but rather "termination without just cause". On the basis of this fact, we say that the dismissal of a worker under an employment contract of indefinite duration will be qualified as abusive when it has no connection with the worker's aptitude or conduct, or with the operating requirements of the company, establishment or department, or with the needs of the business.

In other words, if the dismissal is based on one of the indicative facts listed in article 32 paragraph 2 of the French Labor Code, facts to which we referred earlier in our work and which distinguish between unfair dismissal and dismissal that is not unfair, and given the purely enunciative nature of the facts that do not constitute valid grounds for dismissal. We can say that not every fact that a reasonable man, a family man, could invoke to justify dismissal would be grounds for dismissal.[43]

The option taken by the legislator is a dangerous one, as it could lead to contradictory court rulings. This is a source of legal uncertainty.

To protect employees from losing their jobs, statutory notice is not enough. Termination of the employment contract by the employer must be based on an objective, real and serious cause.

In LUWENYAMA's view, it is the theory of abuse of right that must be retained in order to reconcile and invariably protect the worker's right to stable employment and the well-being of the company[44] .

No-one can remain in a contractual employment relationship against their will, but they can leave it only if they meet objective and indisputable criteria, or if they base their departure on a sufficiently serious reason to justify it.

In the following paragraph, we'll explain the difference between unfair dismissal and unlawful dismissal.

§2 . Differentiation from unlawful dismissal

It is often difficult to differentiate between unfair dismissal and unlawful dismissal, as the issue is not yet clearly defined in our country. The courts equate unfair dismissal with unlawful dismissal, and often order the

---

[43] Read more about BUKA eka ngoy
[44] LUWEENYAMA, op.cit

employer to pay damages.[45]

This is not the case under French law, since Article L 122-14-4 of the French Labor Code stipulates that the dismissal of an employee tainted by a formal irregularity is not null and void, but is sanctioned by the payment of compensation of up to one month's salary[46].

Dismissal is considered abusive when it is not based on a valid reason, whereas dismissal without respect for procedure is illegal.[47] This practice is justified by the fact that illegal dismissal can only result in the employer being ordered to pay damages[48]. The other approach, as we shall see, gives the unjustly dismissed worker the right to reinstatement, with damages payable only if this right is waived.

For example, the dismissal of a trade union delegate convicted of embezzlement by his employer, without prior authorization from the labor inspectorate[49], was deemed illegal. On the other hand, the dismissal of a person accused of theft was considered abusive, even though it had been established that he was on a mission abroad[50] when the object disappeared.

Now that we've covered the basics of unfair dismissal, the next section looks at the consequences it entails.

---

[45] MASANGA PHOBA, O Op.cit.
[46] MASANGA PHOBA, op.cit.
[47] MASANGA PHOBA,op.cit
[48] Art 65 al 3 of the Labor Code
[49] MASANGA PHOBA, op.cit.
[50] MMASANGA PHOBA PHOBA, op.cit.

SECTION 2. EFFECTS OF UNFAIR DISMISSAL

These effects will be indicated first with regard to the employer, then with regard to the employee.

§1 . Effects on the employer

In the event of unfair dismissal, the employer is obliged to reinstate the employee if he chooses to do so. Otherwise, he will be liable for damages calculated taking into account the nature of the services rendered, the employee's seniority in the company, his age, and any rights he may have acquired[51] . of the nature of the 63 of the Labor Code provides for two effects with regard to the employer which are rights to the worker: reinstatement of the worker within the company or, failing this, payment of damages set by the labor court calculated taking into account, in particular, the nature of the services engaged, the worker's seniority in the company, his age and rights acquired in any capacity whatsoever.

It is important to note that the legislator limits the amount of these damages to a maximum of 36 months' remuneration[52] .

§2 . Effects on the employee

What was an obligation for the employer becomes a right for the

---

[51] Art 63 1 of the Labor Code
[52] Article 63 al 1 of the Labor Code

employee: the right to reinstatement or, failing that, to damages.

A. damages law

In practical terms, everything has already been said about the damages to which an unfairly dismissed employee is entitled. We will confine ourselves to mentioning one fact which we feel is important, namely the legislator's limitation on the amount of damages.

In fact, it cannot exceed 36 months of the last remuneration[53]

.

In the absence of the assessment elements listed in article 63 paragraph 1, and in particular when the employee is unable to provide proof of his or her advantages within the company (salary and other benefits), or of his or her seniority, the court may resort to an assessment of ex aequo and bono interests. This method is strictly exceptional[54] .

However, insofar as this has been provided for in the employment contract or collective agreement, the employee may, in addition to damages, be entitled to severance pay.[55]

B. The right to reinstatement

It's about putting the worker back where he or she was before being unfairly dismissed.

---

[53] Article 63 al 2 of the Labor Code
[54] MASANGA PHOBA, op.cit p.81
[55] MASANGA PHOBA,op.cit p.82

A worker who has been unfairly dismissed can choose to be reinstated, to return to the job he or she was doing. In our opinion, this option can have both positive and negative aspects.

1. The positive side

The positive side of reintegration lies in the fact that the worker escapes unemployment by recovering his or her job, which is a major advantage, firstly because for several decades now, the world of employment has offered very limited hiring opportunities; and secondly because the benefit of damages presents a very temporary economic and financial need when we take into account the persistent erosion of our currency.

2. The downside

As we said earlier, the employment contract takes the individual into account, without which the relationship between worker and employer will be ephemeral. Once the worker is back on the job, the employer will always tend to come up with tricks to create an unhealthy working climate that will drive the worker to resign.

Thus, the negative aspect outweighs the positive aspect of reinstatement, which confirms the research we carried out at the BANDUNDU High Court and Court of Appeal.

CONCLUSION

Salaried work is of great importance in any society. It enables us to produce and pay for a wide range of services.

So it's hardly surprising that it's subject to rigorous regulation, which is designed to safeguard all the interests involved - those of workers and employers alike.

However, it has to be said that this fair balance in the relationship between the parties to an employment contract is not rigorously guaranteed when it comes to the dissolution of that contract. The employee's status is far superior to that of the employer.

In fact, all he needs is a short notice period to leave the company, without any further consideration of his own.

For him, his departure is always legitimate and never abusive, although it can also be detrimental to the employer. And that's not all: another great favor is granted to the employee who can disorganize a job within the company.

In fact, in order to look for another job, if it is the employee who has taken the initiative to terminate the contract, the employee is entitled to one day per week during the notice period, then his or her entitlement as a whole or by half-day and paid at full salary[55] .

This is our observation, which calls for a rebalancing of rights between workers and employers when it comes to terminating employment contracts[56] .

These are the main themes of this scientific ballad.[56]

[5655] Art 65 al 2 of the Labor Code
[56] BUKA eka Ngoy, op.cit.

BIBLIOGRAPHY

I. CONSTITUTIONAL, LEGAL AND REGULATORY TEXTS

1. DRC Constitution of February 18, 2006 as amended to date

2. Decree of July 30, 1888 on contracts or conventional obligations

3. Ordinance-law n°68/491 of 2O/12/1962

4. Law n°87/010 August 1987 on the Family Code as amended and supplemented to date

5. Act no. 15/015-2002 on the Labour Code, as amended and supplemented to date

6. Ministerial order no. 062/cab/PVPM/ETPS of July 22, 2011 establishing the form, proof and visa of the employment contract.

II. WORKS

1. LEFEBVRE .F, droit du travail et la sécurité sociale, Mémonto, pratique sociale, 1991 n°2675

2. LUWENYAMA LULE, précis de droit du travail zaïrois, ed.lule, kin, 1989

3. MUKADI BONYI, litiges individuels du travail, chroniques de jurisprudence (1980-1995), collection information juridiques, KIN, 1997

4. NSOLOTSHI MALANGU, calculating damages for unfair dismissal in open-ended employment contracts, online dissertation.

5. NZANGI B., <u>guide juridique des employeurs et des travailleurs dans le processus de la rupture du contrat de travail pour faute lourde</u>, imprimerie saint Paul, limite, KINSHASA, 1996

III. <u>COURSES</u>

1. BUKA eKa NGOY, Commercial company law, first degree, Faculty of Law, Uniband, 2O15-2016

2. DARANAS STYLIANI, <u>Droit du travail et de la sécurité sociale</u>, tome I, 1ere licence Droit, UNIKIN, 1999-2000

3. KABASELE NICOLAS, Droit civil : les obligations, G2 faculté Droit Uniband, 2012

4. KIYALA, course in labour law and social security, 1st law degree, UNIBAND, 2015

5. KUMBU ki NGIMBI, Labour law, teaching manual, Congolese universities, Kinshasa, January 2010

6. LANDU <u>urbain, licenciement abusif en droit congolais</u>, dissertation, University of Bukavu, 2010 unpublished

7. LENZA petronnelle, IRS handout notes, G2 Informatique G2, ISSD

8. MASANGA phoba, labour law, 1ere licence Droit, UNIKIN ,2010

9. First employment seminar, Kinshasa 7/2/2011, ed. Kazi, how to keep a job

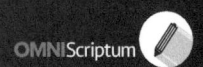

Printed by Books on Demand GmbH, Norderstedt / Germany